TEACH YOURS...

GUI...

SON...

To access online content visit:
www.halleonard.com/mylibrary

Enter Code
4216-6218-8947-3842

ISBN 978-1-4950-4950-7

HAL•LEONARD®
CORPORATION

7777 W. BLUEMOUND RD. P.O. BOX 13819 MILWAUKEE, WI 53213

CONTENTS

ANJI
Paul Simon (Simon & Garfunkel)

Video Lesson – 24 minutes, 2 seconds

Standard Tuning: (low to high) E–A–D–G–B–E
Key of A minor (capo II)

Guitar Tone:

- steel-string or nylon-string acoustic guitar
- light reverb
- capo at 2nd fret

Techniques:

- Fingerpicking: in general, use your thumb to pluck the bass notes on the lower three strings, and your index, middle, and ring fingers to pluck the 3rd, 2nd, and 1st strings, respectively.

- Fingernails, Flesh, and Fingerpicks: there are several ways you can pluck the strings with your fingers. Fingernails sound great and can provide a consistent, clean attack, but you'll need to keep them well-buffed and filed so they are smooth and curved naturally around the fingertips. Some players will use just the flesh of their fingertips to pluck; this has its advantages as well. The sound is less consistent, but warmer and more organic, plus you don't have the nail maintenance. Another alternative are a thumbpick and fingerpicks, similar to a banjo player. These create a consistent sound and don't require upkeep, but do take some time to get used to. On the original recording for this tune, Paul Simon played with a thumbpick and without fingerpicks, using his bare fingers instead.

- Palm Muting: throughout a good portion of the song, the 5th and 6th strings will be palm muted. Rest your pick-hand palm against the strings where they meet the saddle or bridge. The notes should sound somewhat muffled with minimal sustain.

- Hammer-Ons/Pull-Offs: for hammer-ons, strike the first note and then come down forcefully with your fret-hand finger to sound the next note. For the pull-off, strike the first note while also fretting the second note below. Pull off in a slightly downward motion, allowing the second note to ring. Be careful not to sound the higher string with your pull-off finger.

- Thumb-Fretting: wrap your fret-hand thumb over the neck to fret the F note on the 1st fret, 6th string. If you're not comfortable with this technique, you can finger it a different way, but using the thumb is really the best option.

- Open-String Chords: some of the chords in this song involve a mixture of fretted notes and open strings. Make sure to fret these with the tips of your fret-hand fingers, allowing the open strings to ring clearly.

- String Bending: given that the strings are generally thicker on an acoustic, bending can be a real chore, especially around the first three frets where the strings are the tightest. Try to use support fingers when possible. If you're having a lot of trouble, consider putting on a set of lighter strings or tuning down and moving the capo up further.

Anji

Words and Music by Davy Graham

*Slap strings w/ right hand fingers.

BABE, I'M GONNA LEAVE YOU

Led Zeppelin

Video Lesson – 22 minutes, 7 seconds

Standard Tuning: (low to high) E–A–D–G–B–E
Key of A minor

Guitar Tone:

- acoustic guitar or clean tone electric
- light reverb

Chords:

Intro:

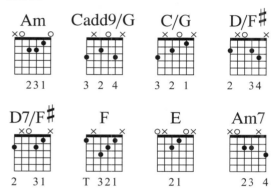

Interludes:

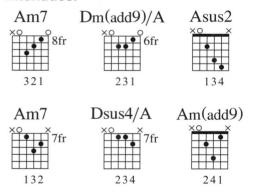

Chorus:

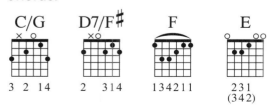

Verse:

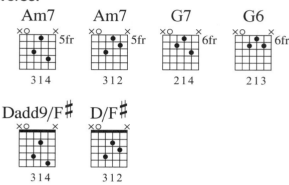

Techniques:

- Fingerpicking: in general, use your thumb to pluck the bass notes on the lower three strings, and your index, middle, and ring fingers to pluck the 3rd, 2nd, and 1st strings, respectively.

- Fingernails, Flesh, and Fingerpicks: there are several ways you can pluck the strings with your fingers. Fingernails sound great and can provide a consistent, clean attack, but you'll need to keep them well-buffed and filed so they are smooth and curved naturally around the fingertips. Some players will use just the flesh of their fingertips to pluck; this has its advantages as well. The sound is less consistent, but warmer and more organic, plus you don't have the nail maintenance. Another alternative are a thumbpick and fingerpicks, similar to a banjo player. These create a consistent sound and don't require upkeep, but do take some time to get used to.

- Thumb-Fretting: wrap your fret-hand thumb over the neck to fret the F note on the 1st fret, 6th string. If you're not comfortable with this technique, you can finger it a different way, but using the thumb is really the best option.

- Open-String Chords: some of the chords in this song involve a mixture of fretted notes and open strings. Make sure to fret these with the tips of your fret-hand fingers, allowing the open strings to ring clearly.

Babe, I'm Gonna Leave You

Words and Music by Anne Bredon, Jimmy Page and Robert Plant

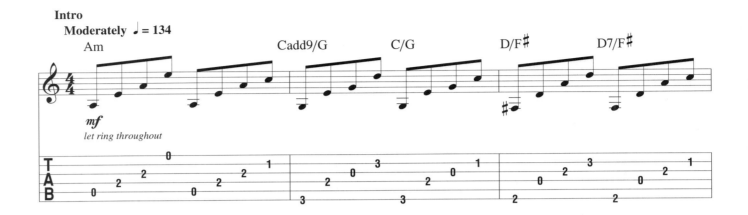

*T = Thumb on 6th str.

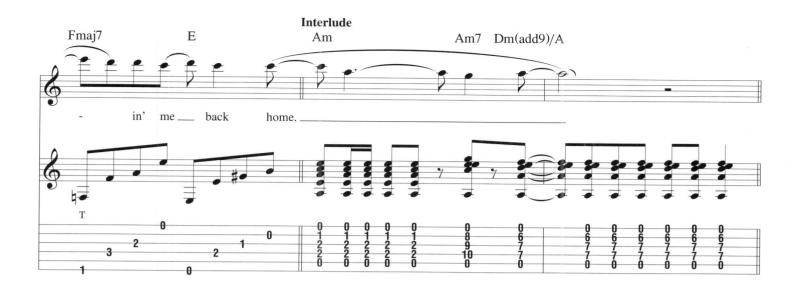

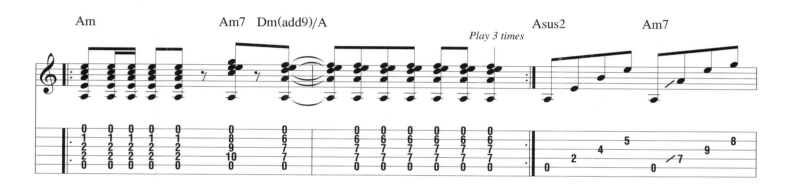

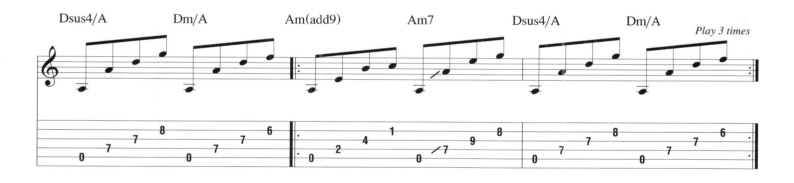

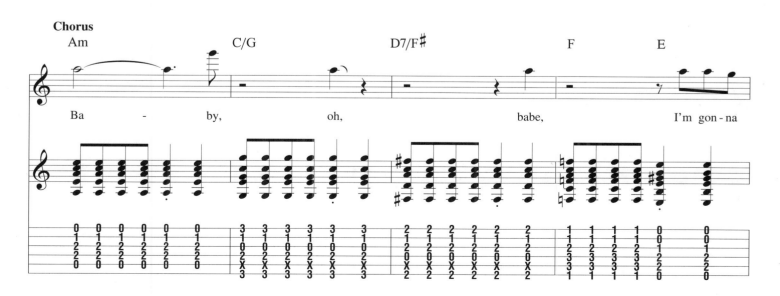

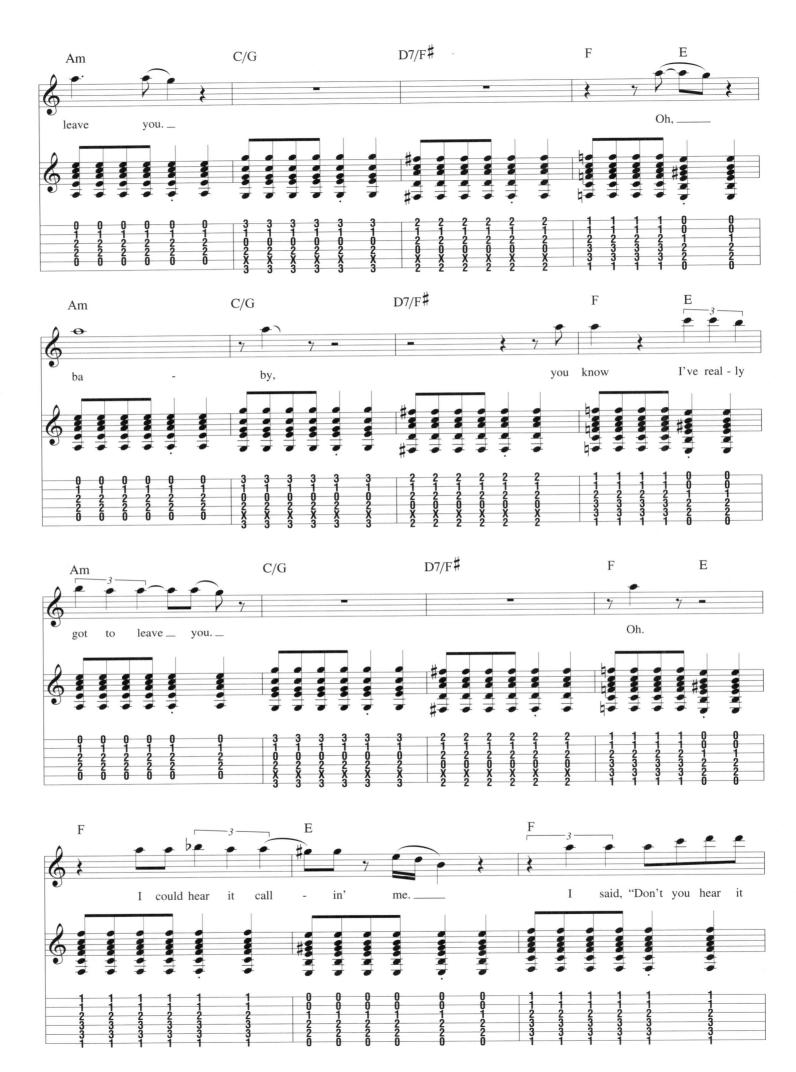

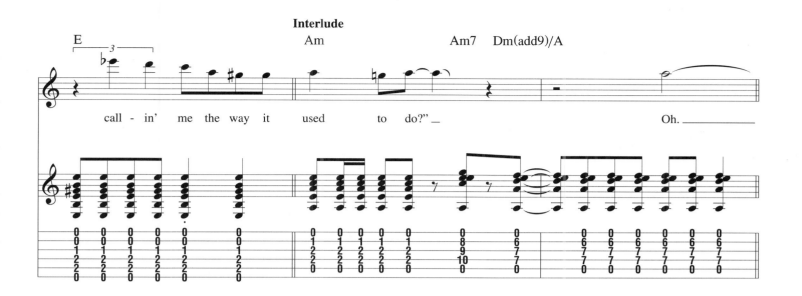

call - in' me the way it used to do?" _ Oh. _____

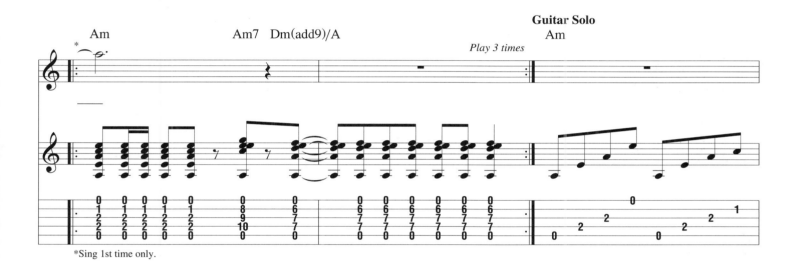

*Sing 1st time only.

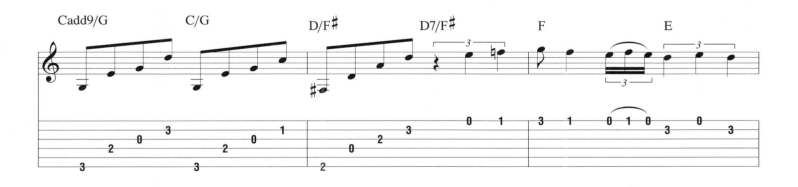

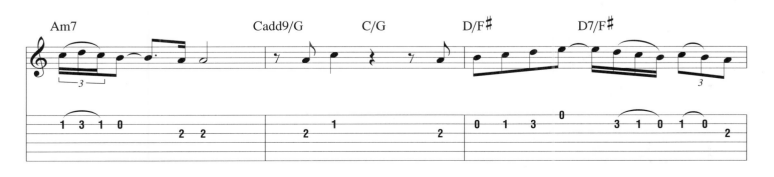

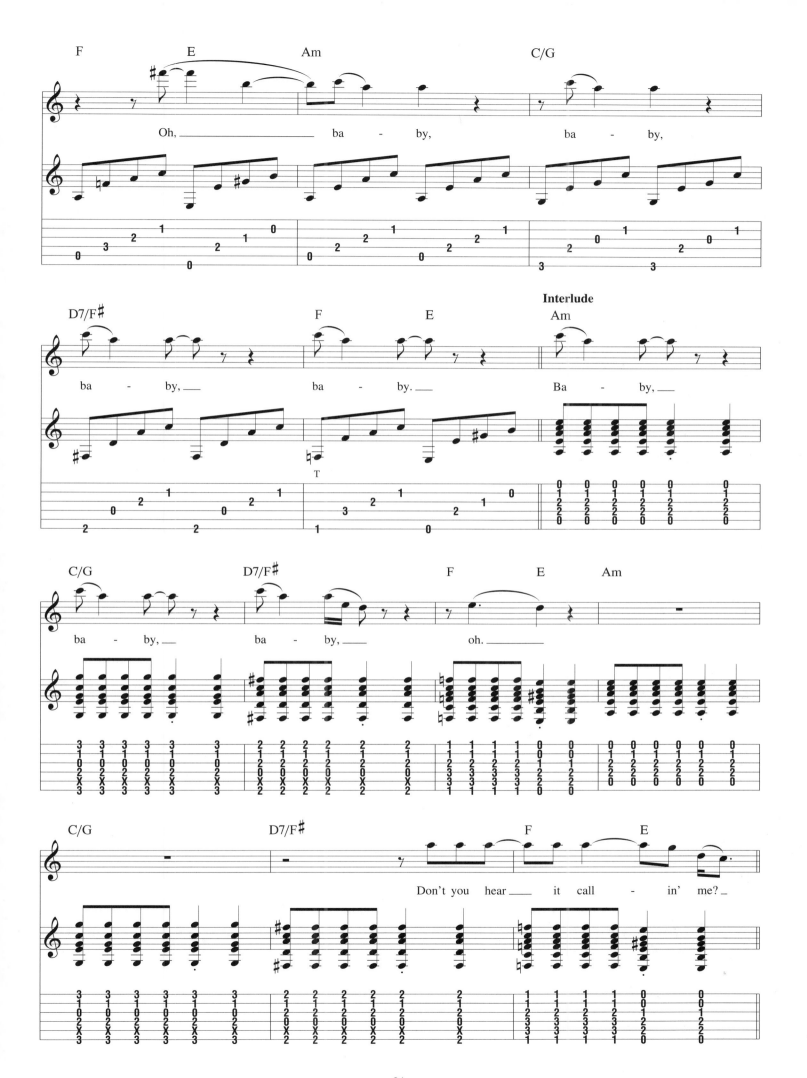

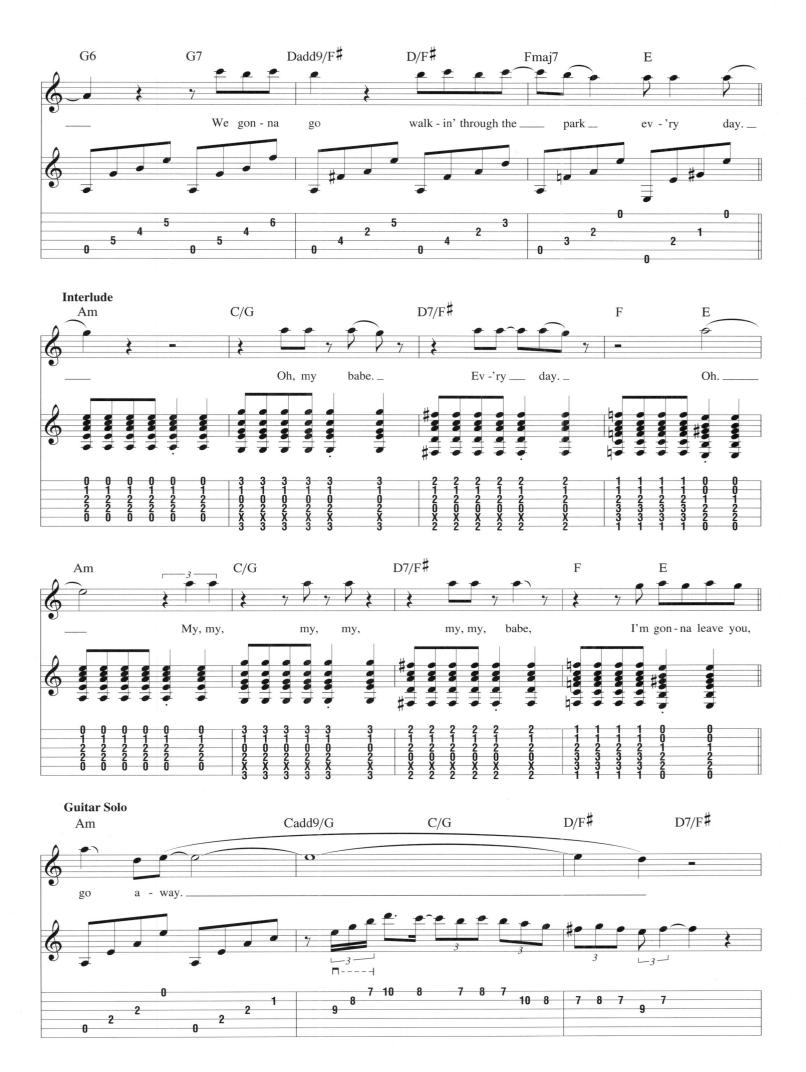

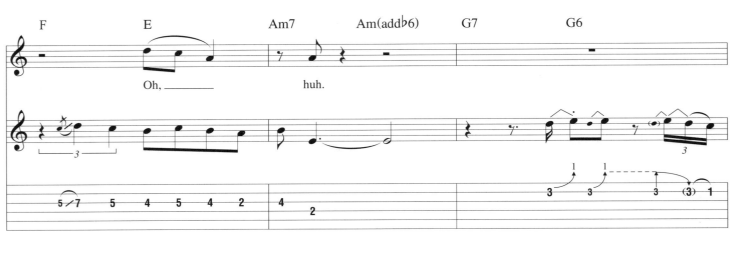

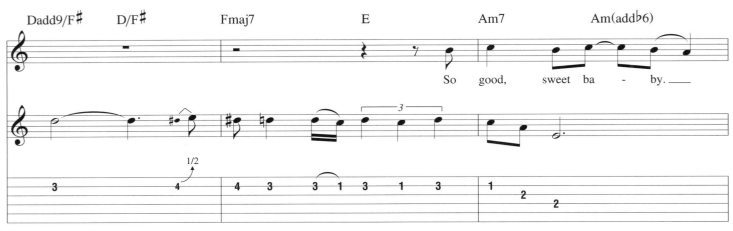

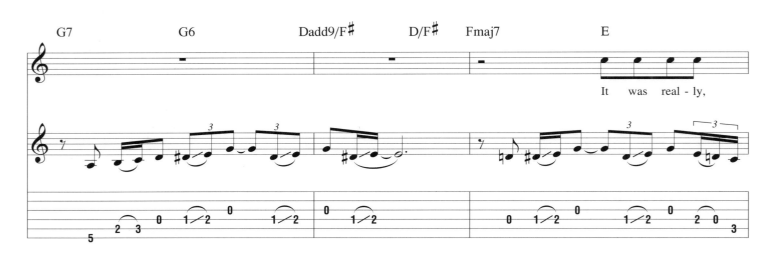

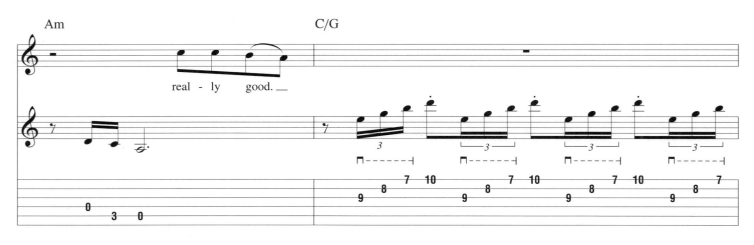

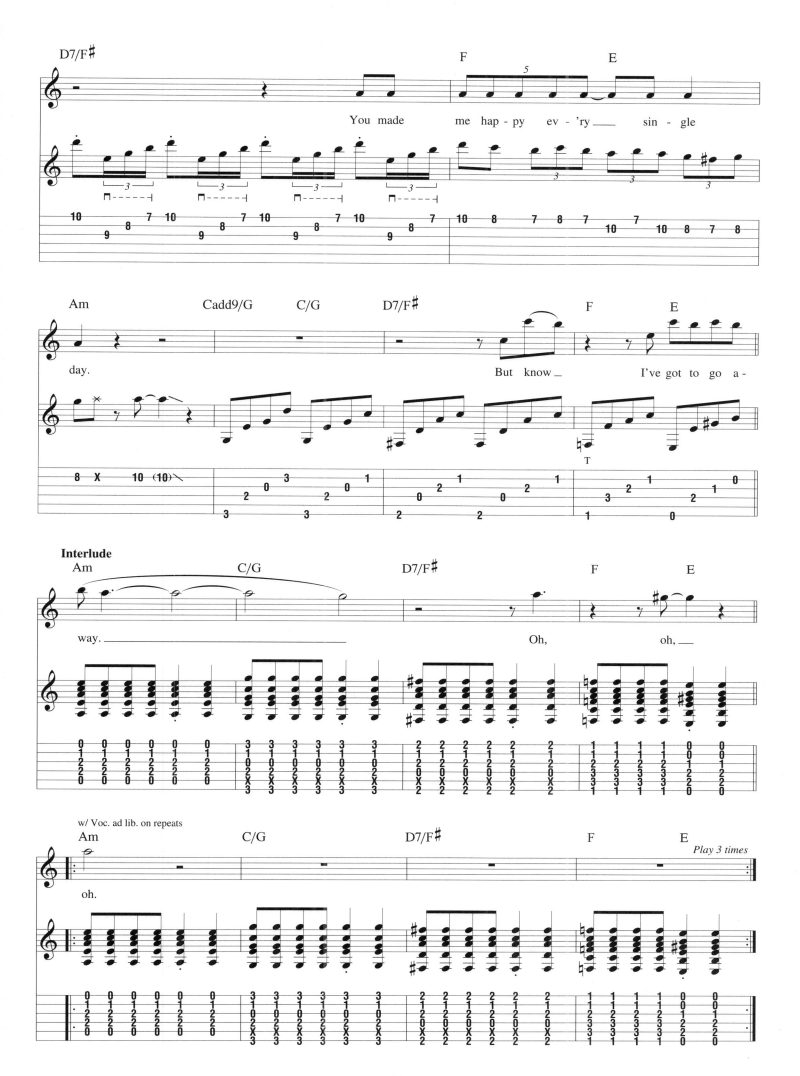

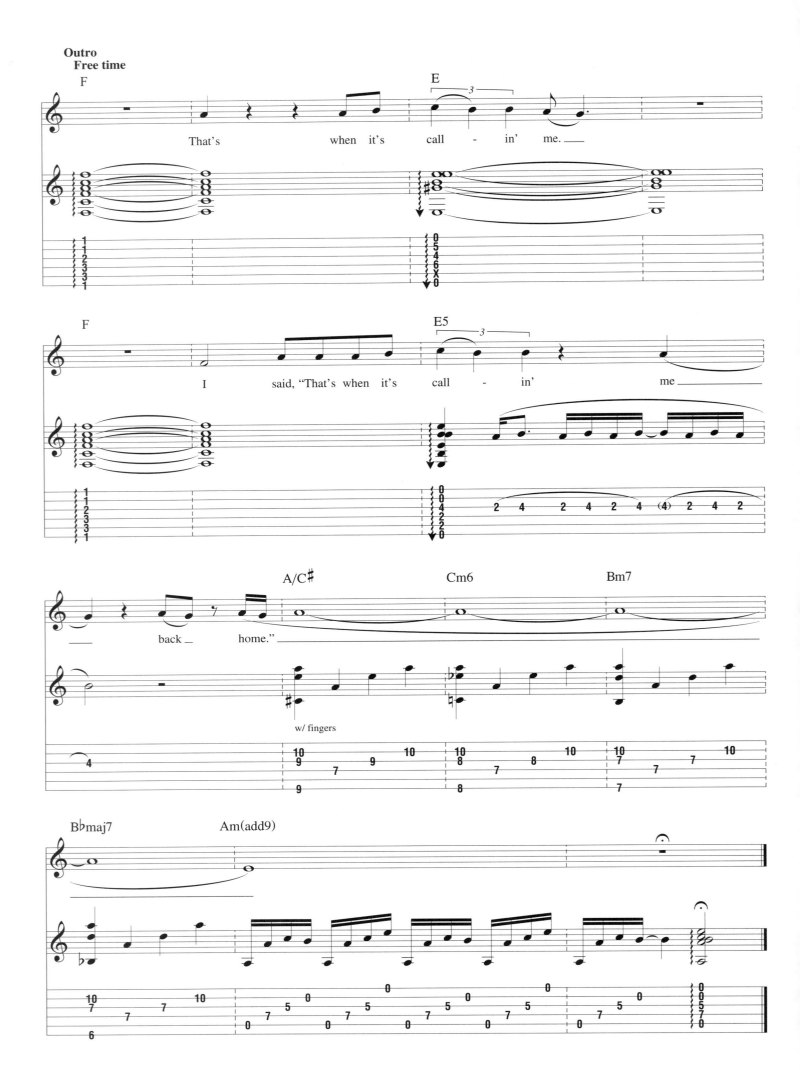

BLACKBIRD
The Beatles

Video Lesson – 12 minutes, 45 seconds

Standard Tuning: (low to high) E–A–D–G–B–E
Key of G

Guitar Tone:

- steel-string or nylon-string acoustic guitar

Techniques:

- Fingerpicking: use the thumb to pick the lower three strings

- Index-Finger Strum: use the index finger as if a pick were attached to it, strumming down and up for the small chords on the inner strings.

- Dyad Slide: hold down the notes of the G/B shape and slide up to the G shape on the 10th and 12th frets, spreading out the fingers enough to form the new dyad.

- Open-String Notes: make sure the open strings are ringing clearly. Fret with the fingertips so you don't accidentally mute any adjacent strings.

- Chromatic Bass Movement: notice how the bass notes climb one fret at a time on the 3rd measure of the Verse. This is a great arranging technique that allows for very smooth-sounding chord transitions. It's also a great fret-hand workout as the shapes get the fingers moving in opposite directions. Practice these moves slowly and make sure both fingers land on the frets at the same time.

- Quick Chord Changes: while not technically considered chords, these dyad shapes are flying by quickly. There is not a lot of time to prepare for the next fingering, so practice landing these shapes accurately. To make these transitions sound smooth, try not to have big gaps in between the changes, allowing the chords to ring as long as possible.

Blackbird

Words and Music by John Lennon and Paul McCartney

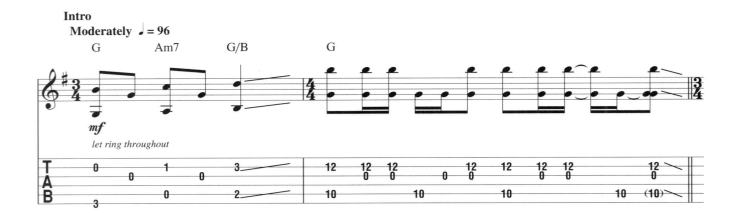

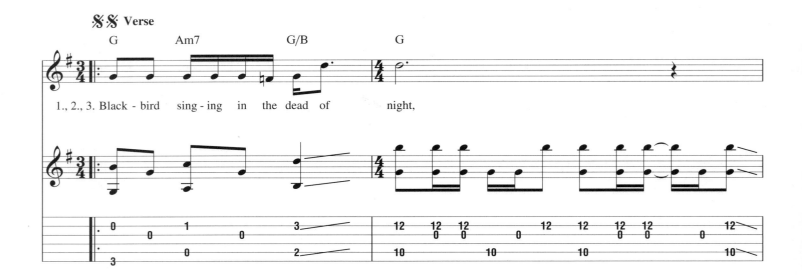

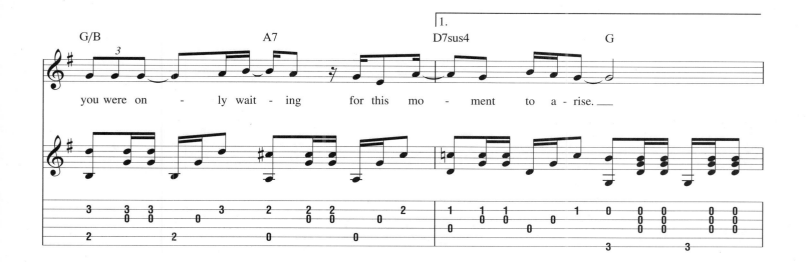

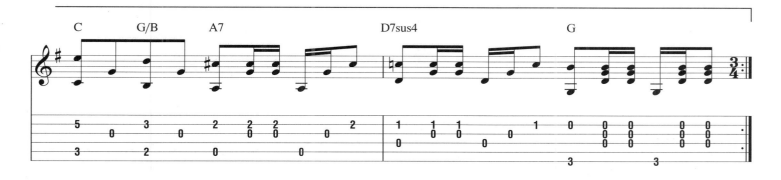

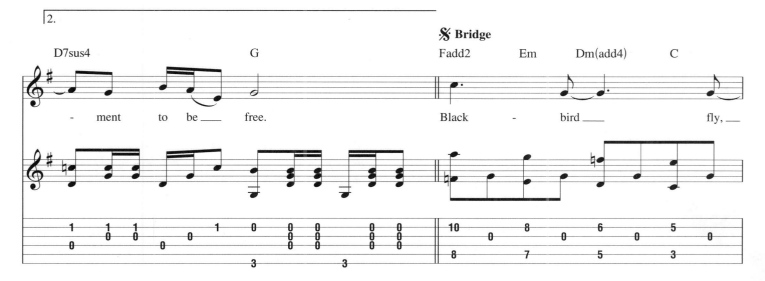

To Coda 1 ⊕

black - bird ___ fly ___
in - to the light ___ of the dark black ___
night. ___

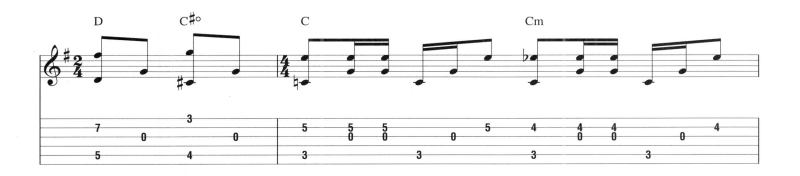

D.S. al Coda 1

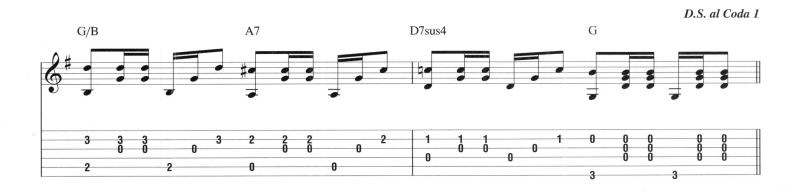

Coda 1

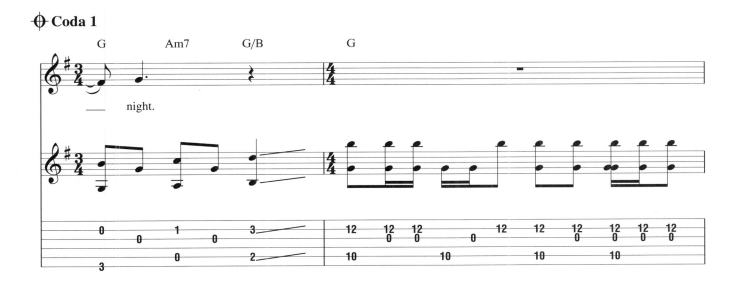

night.

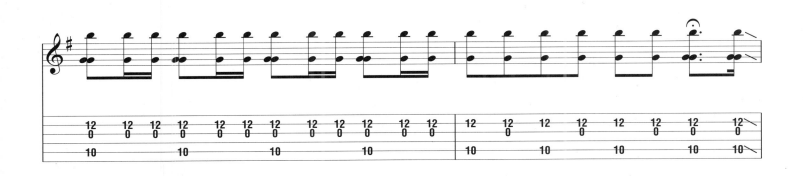

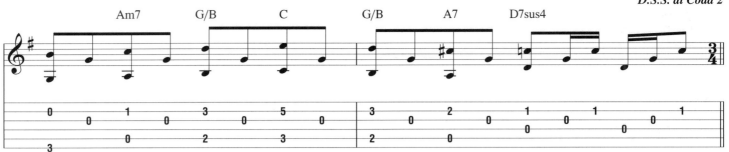

Coda 2

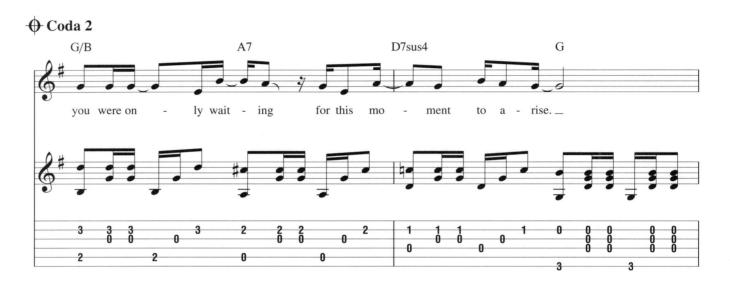

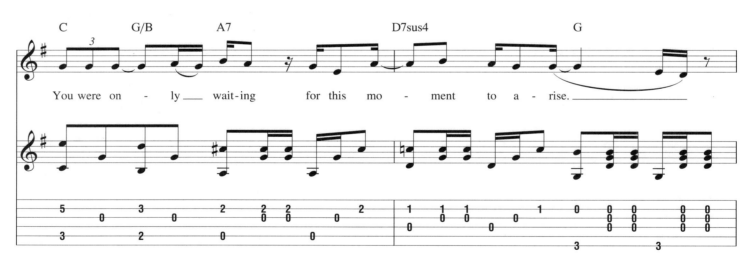

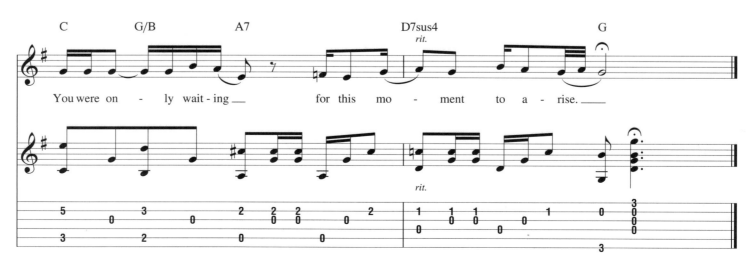

DEE
Randy Rhoads (Ozzy Osbourne)

Video Lesson – 16 minutes, 20 seconds

Standard Tuning: (low to high) E–A–D–G–B–E
Key of D

Guitar Tone:

- steel-string or nylon-string acoustic guitar

Techniques:

- Fingerpicking: in general, use your thumb to pluck the bass notes on the lower three strings, and your index, middle, and ring fingers to pluck the 3rd, 2nd, and 1st strings, respectively.

- Classical Style: this piece is performed in a classical baroque style. Strive to keep the bass notes ringing through each phrase instead of cutting them short (unless they are staccato). In general, all notes should ring as long as possible. Listen to classical guitarists to help absorb the style.

- Staccato: notes with a dot over or under them indicate staccato. This means they should be cut short and not allowed to ring out. After the initial attack, use your left and right hands to mute the strings.

- Harmonics: lightly touch the strings directly above the fret wire, without pushing down to the fretboard. Pluck or strum the strings and lift your hand off, allowing the harmonics to ring.

- Arpeggios: there are several arpeggios in this piece. Keep your fret-hand fingers arched so they don't inadvertently bump or mute any other strings. It helps to keep your fret-hand thumb planted on the back of the neck, roughly opposite of your middle finger. This classical position will help keep your fingers arched, while also facilitating the fretting of the dyads that occur throughout as well.

- Fingernails, Flesh, and Fingerpicks: there are several ways you can pluck the strings with your fingers. Fingernails sound great and can provide a consistent, clean attack, but you'll need to keep them well-buffed and filed so they are smooth and curved naturally around the fingertips. Some players will use just the flesh of their fingertips to pluck; this has its advantages as well. The sound is less consistent, but warmer and more organic, plus you don't have the nail maintenance. Another alternative are a thumbpick and fingerpicks, similar to a banjo player. These create a consistent sound and don't require upkeep, but do take some time to get used to.

Dee

Music by Randy Rhoads

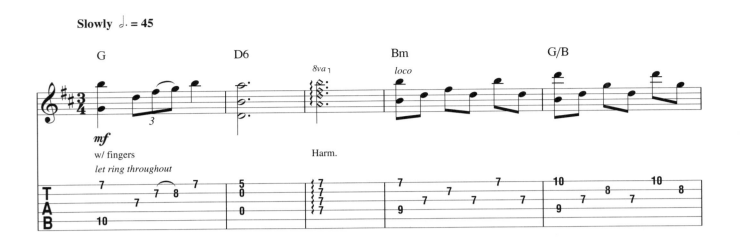

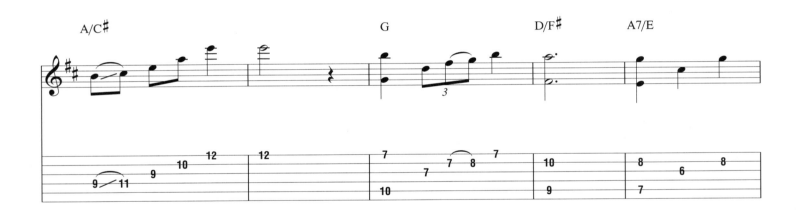

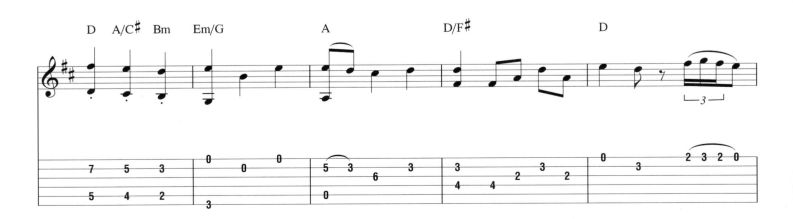

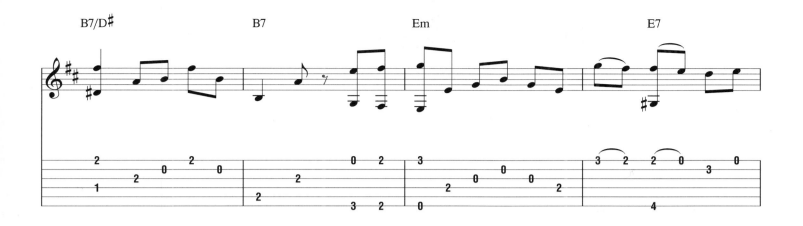

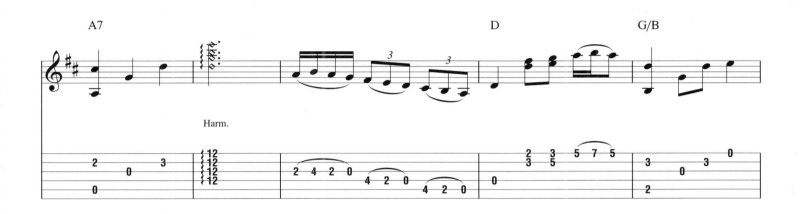

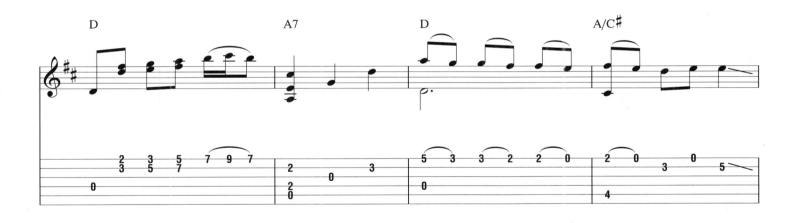

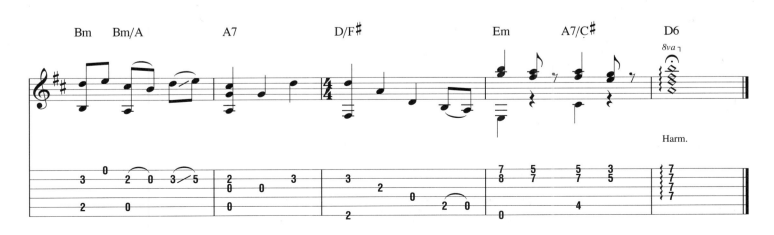

DUST IN THE WIND
Kansas

Video Lesson – 19 minutes, 11 seconds

Standard Tuning: (low to high) E–A–D–G–B–E
Key of C

Guitar Tone:

- steel-string or nylon-string acoustic guitar

- light reverb

Chords:

Intro:

C   Cmaj7   Cadd9   Asus2

32 1   32   32 4   23

Asus4   Am

234   231

Verse:

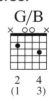

G/B   G   Dm7

2   4   3   2 1 1
(1   3)

Chorus:

D/F♯   Am/G

1   23   4   231

Interlude:

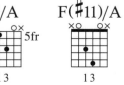

Am(add9)   G/A   F(♯11)/A   F6(♯11)/A

31   13   13   131

Outro:

Asus4(♭13)

2341

Techniques:

- Fingerpicking: follow the suggested pick-hand fingering. The pattern, referred to as "Travis picking," is consistent throughout the song. Start off slowly and pay close attention to the rhythms. Build speed gradually but don't sacrifice accuracy.

- Fingernails, Flesh, and Fingerpicks: there are several ways you can pluck the strings with your fingers. Fingernails sound great and can provide a consistent, clean attack, but you'll need to keep them well-buffed and filed so they are smooth and curved naturally around the fingertips. Some players will use just the flesh of their fingertips to pluck; this has its advantages as well. The sound is less consistent, but warmer and more organic, plus you don't have the nail maintenance. Another alternative are a thumbpick and fingerpicks, similar to a banjo player. These create a consistent sound and don't require upkeep, but do take some time to get used to.

- Open-String Chords: some of the chords in this song involve a mixture of fretted notes and open strings. Make sure to fret these with the tips of your fret-hand fingers, allowing the open strings to ring clearly.

Dust in the Wind

Words and Music by Kerry Livgren

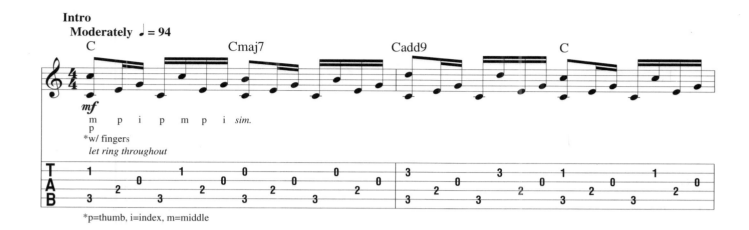

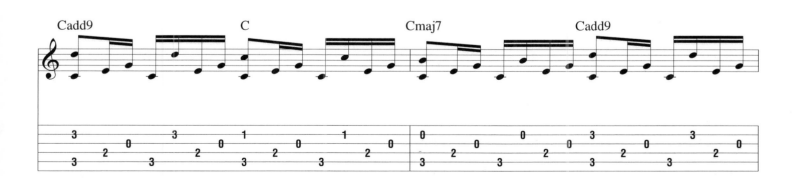

Verse

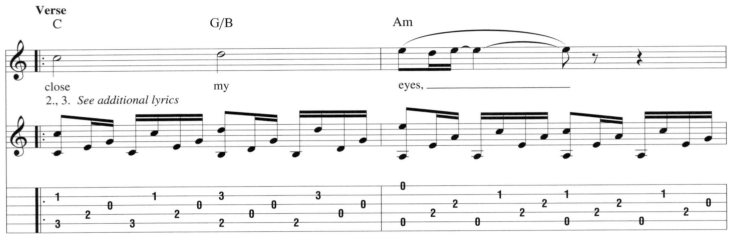

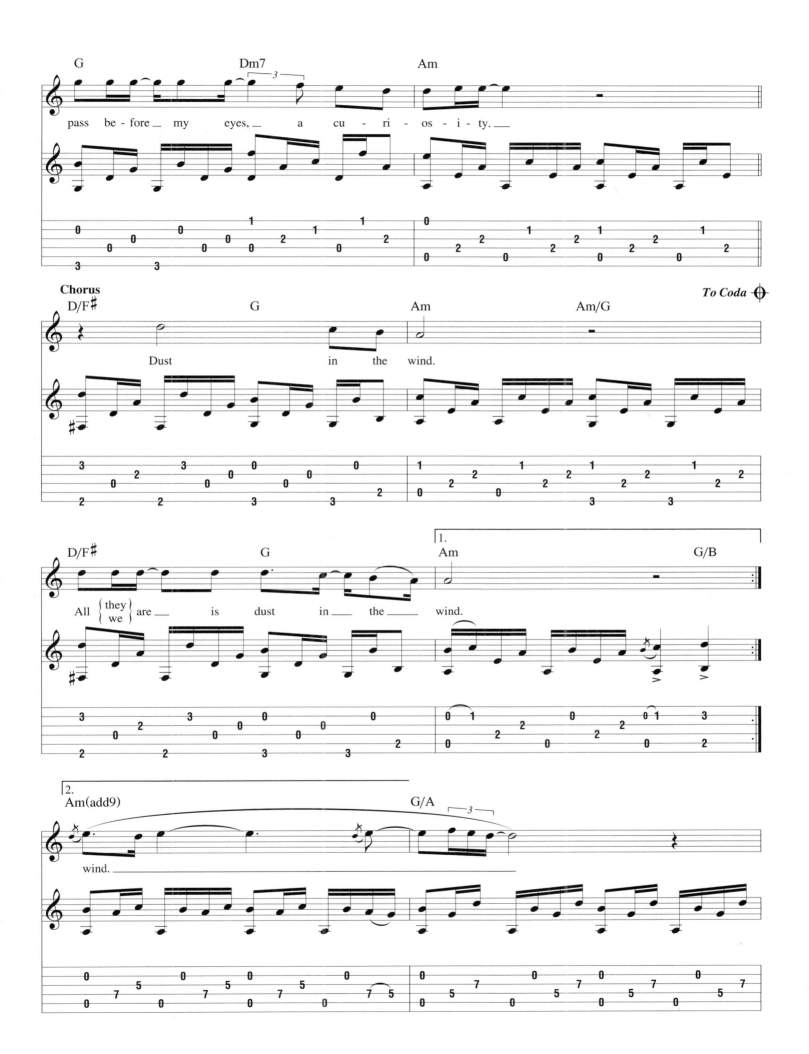

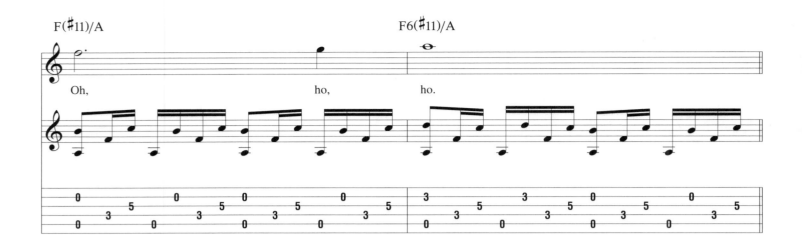

Oh, ho, ho.

Interlude

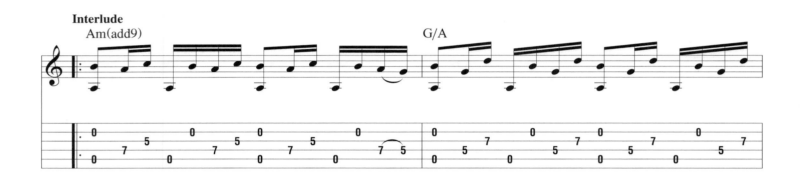

2nd time, D.C. al Coda

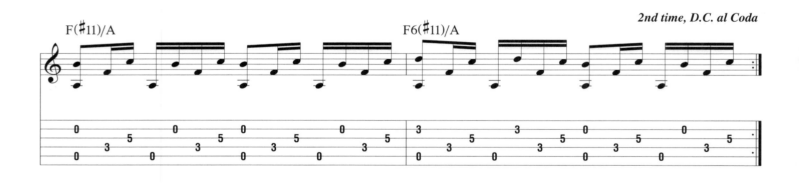

⊕ Coda

All we are __ is dust in __ the wind. __

(All we are __ is dust in __ the

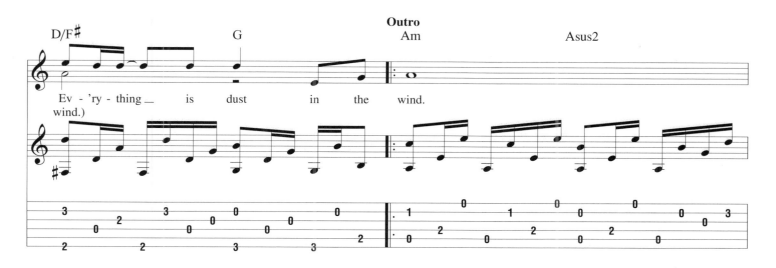

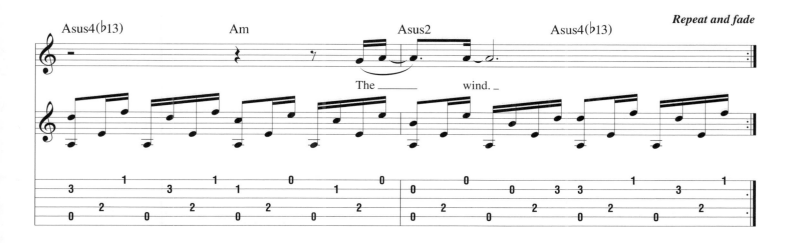

Additional Lyrics

2. Same old song.
   Just a drop of water in an endless sea.
   All we do
   Crumbles to the ground though we refuse to see.

3. Now don't hang on,
   Nothing lasts forever but the earth and sky.
   It slips away
   And all your money won't another minute buy.

FIRE AND RAIN
James Taylor

Video Lesson – 17 minutes, 18 seconds

Standard Tuning: (low to high) E–A–D–G–B–E
Key of A (capo III)

Guitar Tone:

- steel-string or nylon-string acoustic guitar
- light reverb
- capo at 3rd fret

Chords:

Intro:

A	G/E	D	A
2 1 1	2 1 1	1 3 2	1 2 3

E	Gmaj7
2 3 1	2 3 1

Chorus:

Bm7	A7sus2	Asus2
1 1 3 2	2	2 3

Techniques:

- **Fingerpicking:** in general, use your thumb to pluck the bass notes on the lower three strings, and your index, middle, and ring fingers to pluck the 3rd, 2nd, and 1st strings, respectively.

- **Fingernails, Flesh, and Fingerpicks:** there are several ways you can pluck the strings with your fingers. Fingernails sound great and can provide a consistent, clean attack, but you'll need to keep them well-buffed and filed so they are smooth and curved naturally around the fingertips. Some players will use just the flesh of their fingertips to pluck; this has its advantages as well. The sound is less consistent, but warmer and more organic, plus you don't have the nail maintenance. Another alternative are a thumbpick and fingerpicks, similar to a banjo player. These create a consistent sound and don't require upkeep, but do take some time to get used to.

- **Slides:** strike the first note, keep pressure on the string, and slide smoothly to the next indicated fret. Too little pressure and the note will die; too much pressure and it will be hard to slide. It's all about finesse; you've got to find that happy medium.

- **Hammer-Ons/Pull-Offs:** for hammer-ons, strike the first note and then come down forcefully with your fret-hand finger to sound the next note. For the pull-off, strike the first note while also fretting the second note below. Pull off in a slightly downward motion, allowing the second note to ring. Be careful not to sound any other strings with your pull-off finger.

- **Open-String Chords:** some of the chords in this song involve a mixture of fretted notes and open strings. Make sure to fret these with the tips of your fret-hand fingers, allowing the open strings to ring clearly.

- **Accented Strums:** for the accented notes (>), be sure to strum those a bit harder.

Fire and Rain
Words and Music by James Taylor

Capo III

Intro
Slowly ♩ = 77

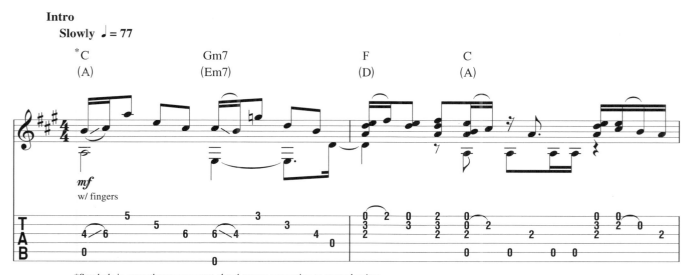

*Symbols in parentheses represent chord names respective to capoed guitar.
Symbols above reflect actual sounding chords. Capoed fret is "0" in tab.

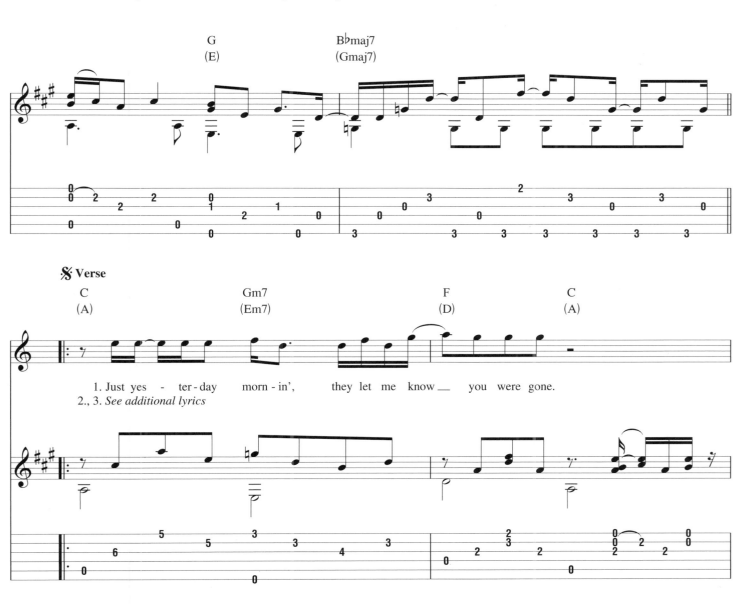

Verse

1. Just yes - ter - day morn - in', they let me know ___ you were gone.
2., 3. *See additional lyrics*

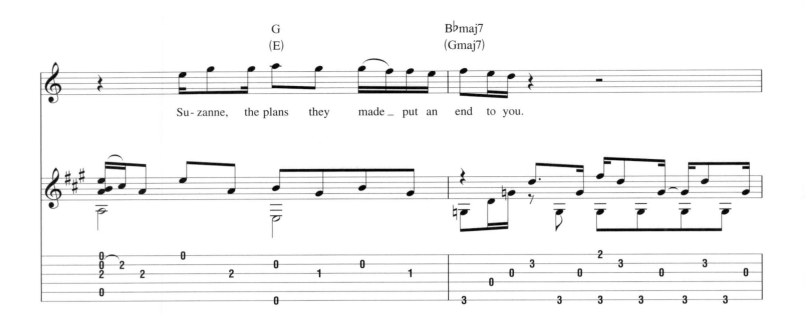

Su - zanne, the plans they made — put an end to you.

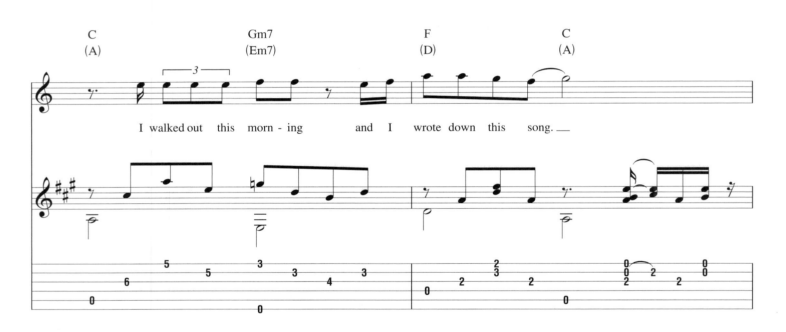

I walked out this morn - ing and I wrote down this song. —

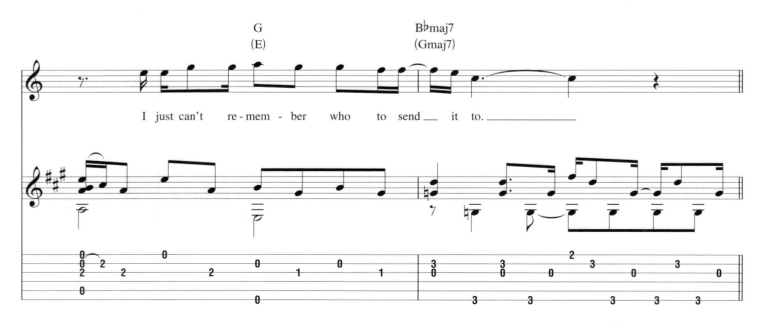

I just can't re - mem - ber who to send — it to. _____

*Strum chords w/ index finger.

al - ways thought that I'd see you a - gain.

2. Won't you al - ways thought _ that I'd see you a - gain. _

D.S. al Coda

3. Been

Coda

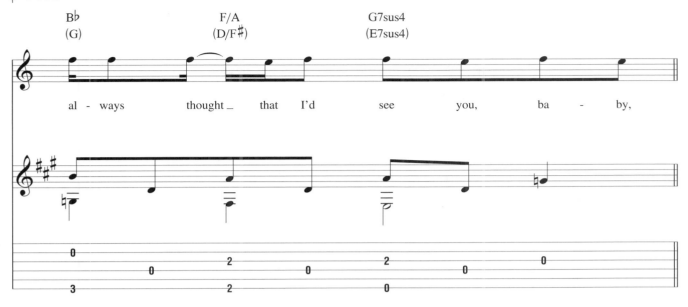

al - ways   thought ‿ that   I'd   see   you,   ba - by,

Outro

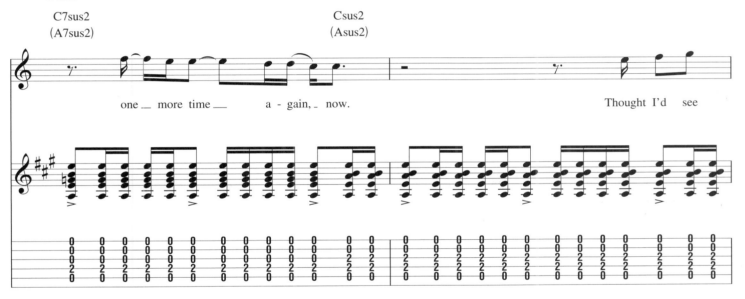

one ‿ more   time ‿   a - gain, ‿ now.   Thought I'd   see

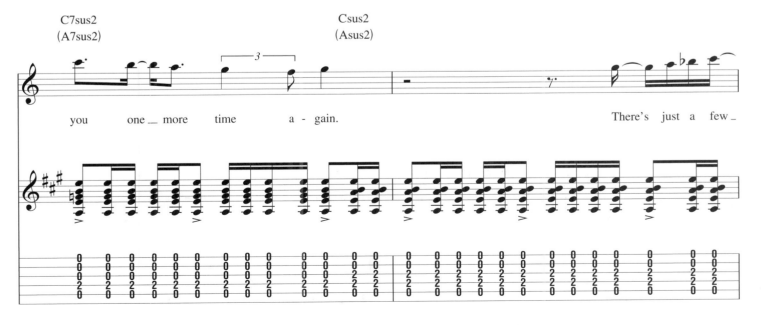

you   one ‿ more   time   a - gain.   There's   just   a   few ‿

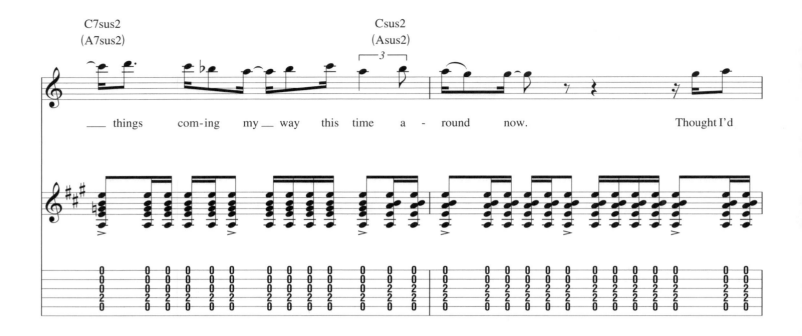

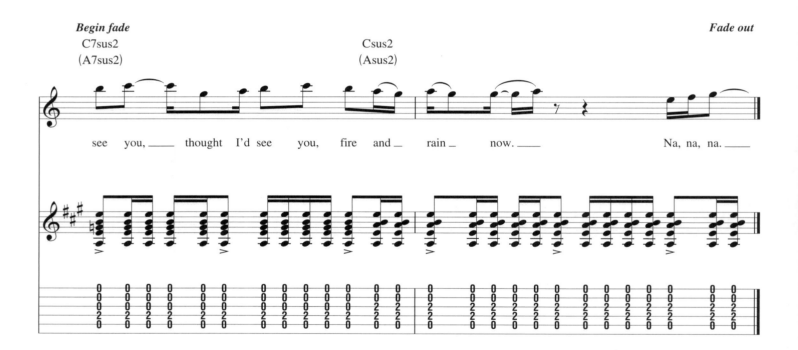

Additional Lyrics

2. Won't ya look down upon me, Jesus,
   Ya gotta help me make a stand.
   You just got to see me through another day.
   My body's achin' and my time is at hand.
   I won't make it any other way.

3. Been walking my mind to an easy time,
   My back turned towards the sun.
   Lord knows when the cold wind blows,
   It'll turn your head around.
   Well, there's hours of time on the telephone line
   To talk about things to come;
   Sweet dreams and flying machines in pieces on the ground.

LITTLE MARTHA
The Allman Brothers Band

Video Lesson – 20 minutes, 27 seconds

Open E Tuning: (low to high) E–B–E–G♯–B–E
Key of E

Guitar Tone:

- steel-string or nylon-string acoustic guitar

- light reverb

Chords:

Section C:

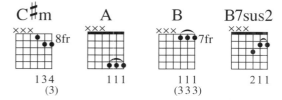

Techniques:

- Fingerpicking: in general, use your thumb to pluck the bass notes on the lower three strings, and your index, middle, and ring fingers to pluck the 3rd, 2nd, and 1st strings, respectively.

- Fingernails, Flesh, and Fingerpicks: there are several ways you can pluck the strings with your fingers. Fingernails sound great and can provide a consistent, clean attack, but you'll need to keep them well-buffed and filed so they are smooth and curved naturally around the fingertips. Some players will use just the flesh of their fingertips to pluck; this has its advantages as well. The sound is less consistent, but warmer and more organic, plus you don't have the nail maintenance. Another alternative are a thumbpick and fingerpicks, similar to a banjo player. These create a consistent sound and don't require upkeep, but do take some time to get used to.

- Hammer-Ons/Pull-Offs: for hammer-ons, strike the first note and then come down forcefully with your fret-hand finger to sound the next note. For the pull-off, strike the first note while also fretting the second note below. Pull off in a slightly downward motion, allowing the second note to ring. Be careful not to sound any other strings with your pull-off finger.

- Open-String Chords: some of the chords in this song involve a mixture of fretted notes and open strings. Make sure to fret these with the tips of your fret-hand fingers, allowing the open strings to ring clearly.

- Harmonics: hold your finger directly over the indicated fret wire and lightly touch the string. Don't press hard enough to fret it. Strike the string and immediately remove your finger. The harmonic should ring, producing a bell-like tone.

- Staccato: staccato means "short," so play these notes and immediately mute the strings by lifting up your fret-hand fingers, bringing some fret-hand fingers down to stop the strings from ringing, or by muting with the pick-hand palm. These notes should have a quick attack and no sustain.

Little Martha

Written by Duane Allman

Open E tuning:
(low to high) E-B-E-G#-B-E

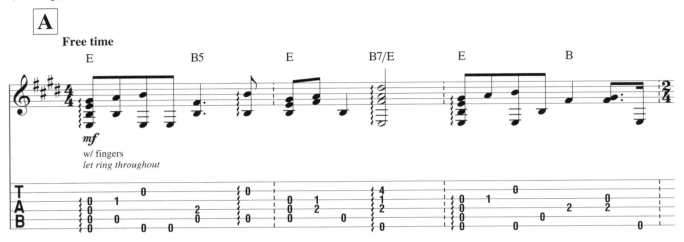

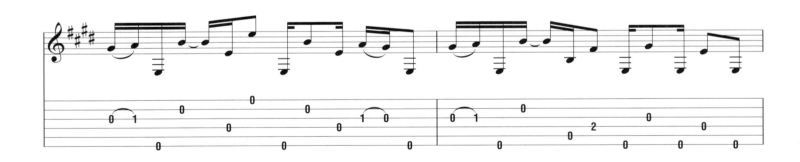

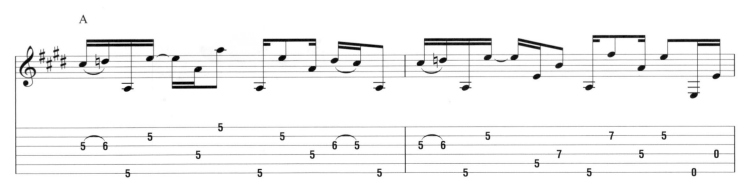

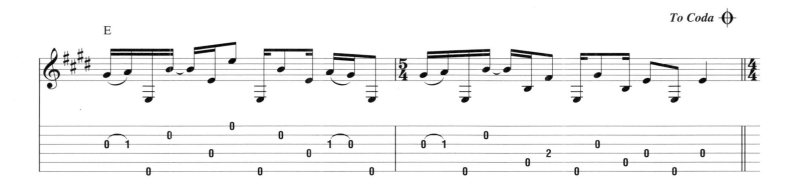

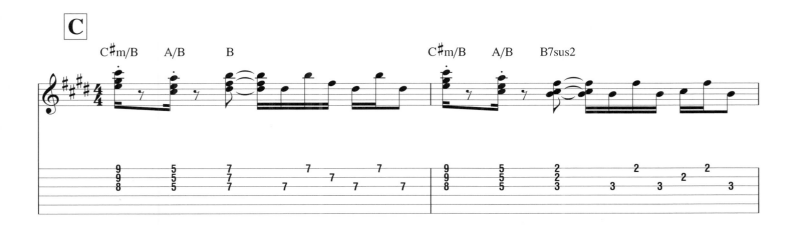

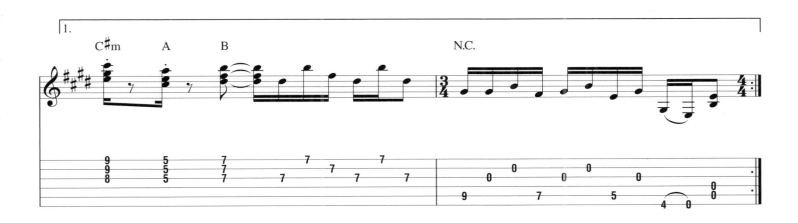

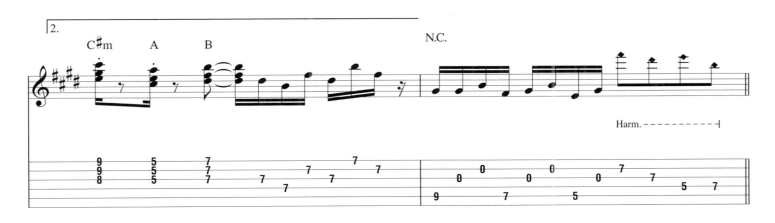

D

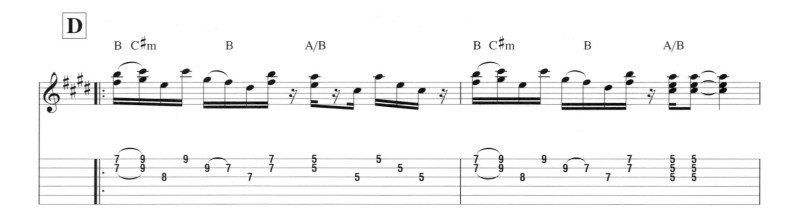

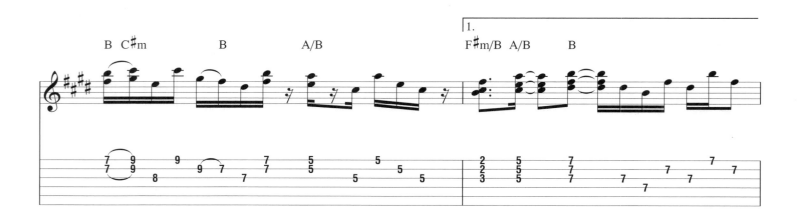

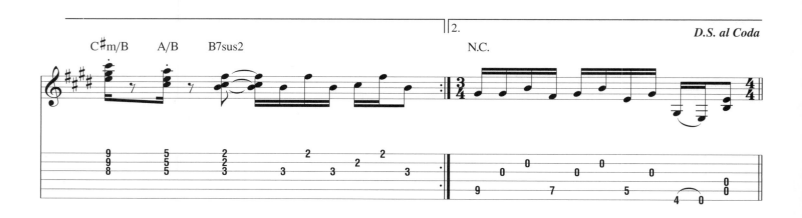

D.S. al Coda

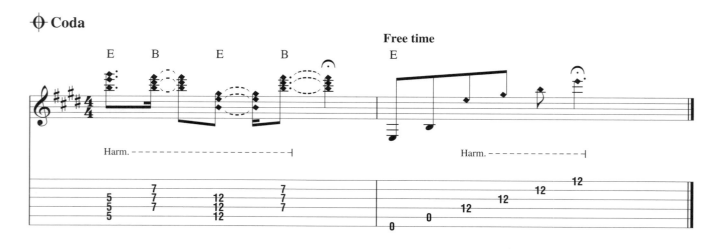

TAKE ME HOME, COUNTRY ROADS
John Denver

Video Lesson – 17 minutes, 1 second

Standard Tuning: (low to high) E–A–D–G–B–E
Key of A

Guitar Tone:

- steel-string acoustic guitar

Chords/Arpeggios:

Intro/Verse:

A   Asus4   F#m   E

1 2 3   1 2 4   1 3 4 1 1 1   2 3 1
(2 3 4)

D

1 3 2

Bridge:

G

2 1   3

Techniques:

- Fingerpicking: in general, use your thumb to pluck the bass notes on the lower three strings, and your index, middle, and ring fingers to pluck the 3rd, 2nd, and 1st strings, respectively. In this song, the thumb will need to pluck the 3rd string as well.

- Fingernails, Flesh, and Fingerpicks: there are several ways you can pluck the strings with your fingers. Fingernails sound great and can provide a consistent, clean attack, but you'll need to keep them well-buffed and filed so they are smooth and curved naturally around the fingertips. Some players will use just the flesh of their fingertips to pluck; this has its advantages as well. The sound is less consistent, but warmer and more organic, plus you don't have the nail maintenance. Another alternative are a thumbpick and fingerpicks, similar to a banjo player. These create a consistent sound and don't require upkeep, but do take some time to get used to.

- Fingerpicking Patterns: you may choose to follow the fingerpicking pattern in the notation exactly, or you could try other patterns as well. Another option is to strum the chords instead of fingerpick, which works great with this song.

Take Me Home, Country Roads

Words and Music by John Denver, Bill Danoff and Taffy Nivert

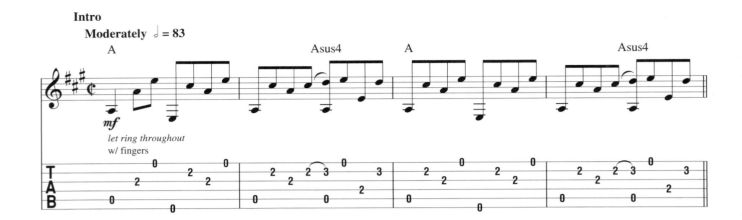

Take _ me home, _____ coun - try roads. _

_____ Take _ me home, _____

_____ coun - try roads. _____

Additional Lyrics

2. All my mem'ries gather 'round her,
   Miner's lady, stranger to blue water.
   Dark and dusty, painted on the sky.
   Misty taste of moonshine, teardrop in my eye.

TEARS IN HEAVEN
Eric Clapton

Video Lesson – 22 minutes, 36 seconds

Standard Tuning: (low to high) E–A–D–G–B–E
Key of A

Guitar Tone:

- nylon-string or steel-string acoustic guitar

- light reverb

Chords:
Intro/Verse:

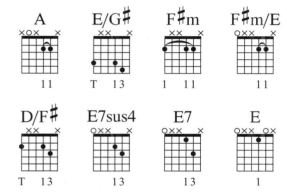

Chorus:

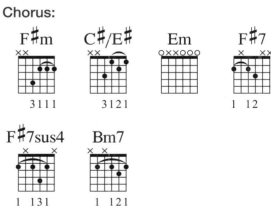

Bridge:

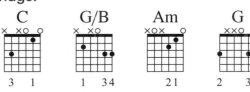

Techniques:

- Fingerpicking: in general, use your thumb to pluck the bass notes on the lower three strings, and your index, middle, and ring fingers to pluck the 3rd, 2nd, and 1st strings, respectively. In this song, the thumb will need to pluck the 3rd string as well.

- Fingernails, Flesh, and Fingerpicks: there are several ways you can pluck the strings with your fingers. Fingernails sound great and can provide a consistent, clean attack, but you'll need to keep them well-buffed and filed so they are smooth and curved naturally around the fingertips. Some players will use just the flesh of their fingertips to pluck; this has its advantages as well. The sound is less consistent, but warmer and more organic, plus you don't have the nail maintenance. Another alternative are a thumbpick and fingerpicks, similar to a banjo player. These create a consistent sound and don't require upkeep, but do take some time to get used to.

- Hammer-Ons/Pull-Offs: for hammer-ons, strike the first note and then come down forcefully with your fret-hand finger to sound the next note. For the pull-off, strike the first note while also fretting the second note below. Pull off in a slightly downward motion, allowing the second note to ring. Be careful not to sound any other strings with your pull-off finger.

- Slides: strike the first note, keep pressure on the string, and slide smoothly to the next indicated fret. Too little pressure and the note will die; too much pressure and it will be hard to slide. It's all about finesse; you've got to find that happy medium.

- Open-String Chords: some of the chords in this song involve a mixture of fretted notes and open strings. Make sure to fret these with the tips of your fret-hand fingers, allowing the open strings to ring clearly.

- Barre Chords: you'll need to barre across three strings for the first two chords in the Chorus. Keep your 1st finger straight and roll slightly to the inside (thumb side) to get a more rigid connection. If you're getting buzzing notes, think more about keeping the finger straight instead of increasing the pressure. Make sure you stay close to the fret to make it easier to hold down the notes.

Tears in Heaven

Words and Music by Eric Clapton and Will Jennings

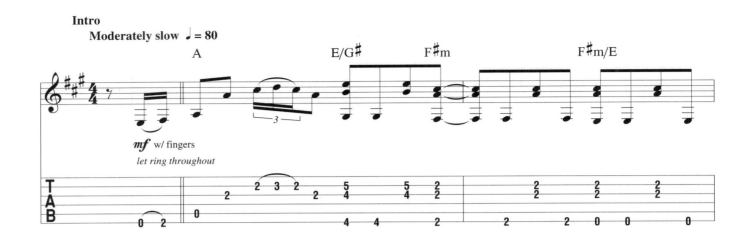

Would it be the same, _____ if I saw you in heav-

Chorus

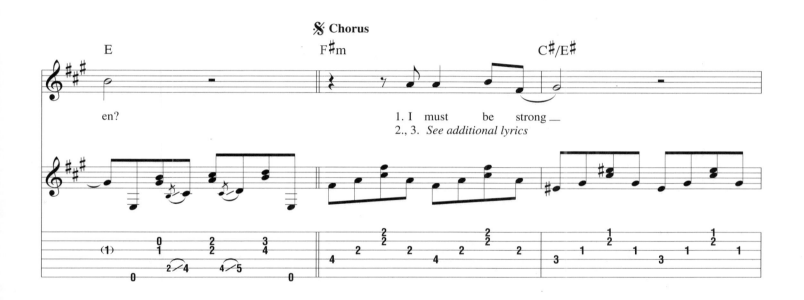

en?

1. I must be strong _____
2., 3. *See additional lyrics*

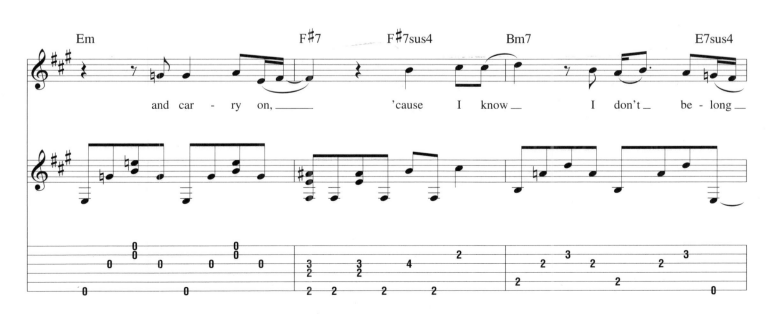

and car - ry on, _____ 'cause I know _____ I don't _____ be - long _____

here in heav - en.

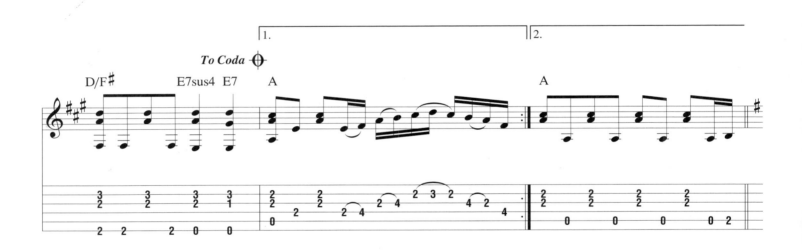

Time _ can bring you down, _ time can bend _ your knees. _

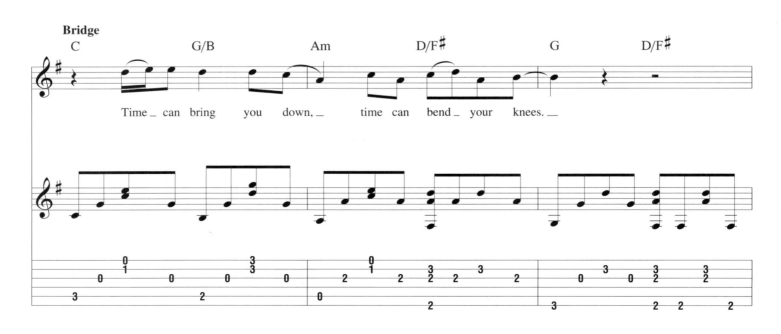

Time — can break your heart, — have you beg - gin' please, —

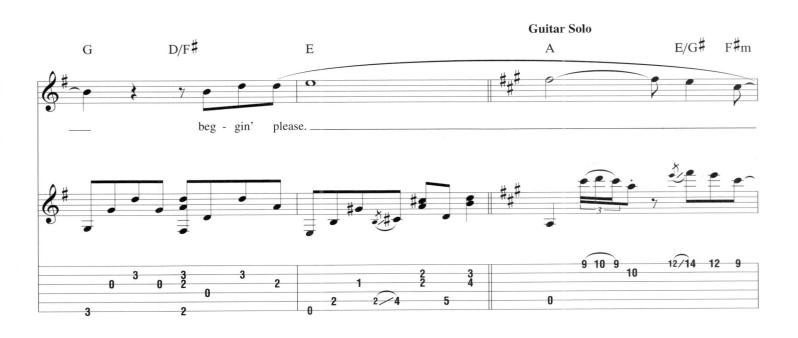

Guitar Solo

— beg - gin' please. _____

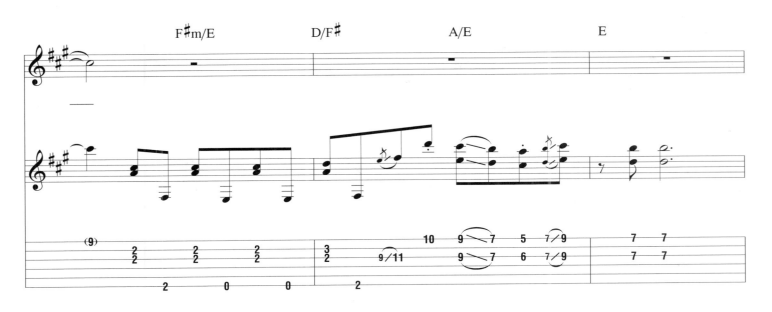

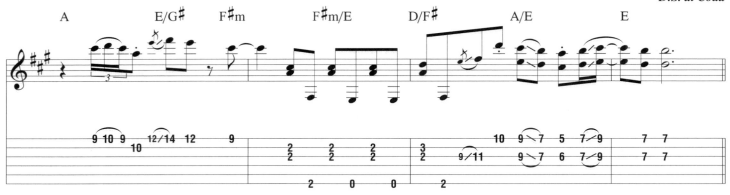

Coda

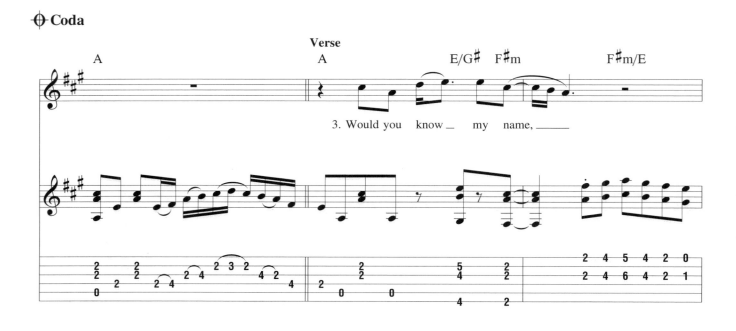

3. Would you know _ my name, _____

if I saw you in heav - en?

Would it be _ the same _

if I saw you in heav - en?

Chorus

I must be strong ___ and car - ry on, ___ 'cause I know ___

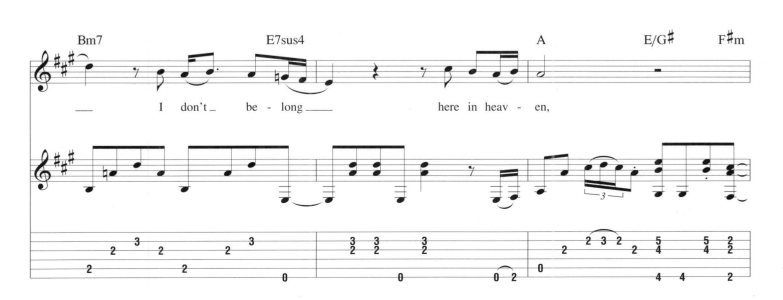

___ I don't ___ be - long ___ here in heav - en,

'cause _ I know I don't _ be - long ___ here in heav - en.

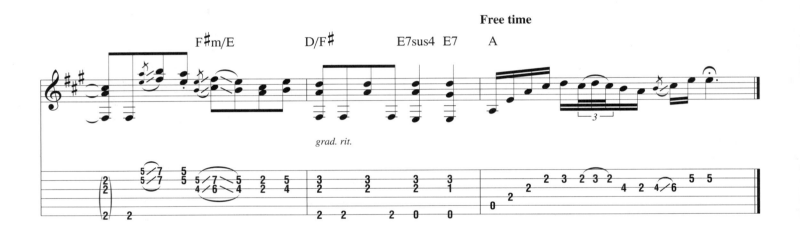

Free time

grad. rit.

Additional Lyrics

2. Would you hold my hand
   If I saw you in heaven?
   Would ya help me stand
   If I saw you in heaven?

Chorus 2. I'll find my way
   Through night and day
   'Cause I know I just can't stay
   Here in heaven.

Chorus 3. Beyond the door
   There's peace, I'm sure,
   And I know there'll be no more
   Tears in heaven.

TIME IN A BOTTLE
Jim Croce

Video Lesson – 11 minutes, 38 seconds

Standard Tuning: (low to high) E–A–D–G–B–E
Key of D minor and D

Guitar Tone:

- steel-string or nylon-string acoustic guitar

Chords/Arpeggios:

Intro/Verse:

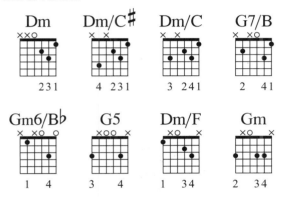

Bridge:

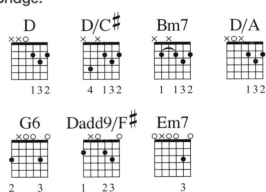

Outro:

Dm(add9)

Techniques:

- Fingerpicking: in general, use your thumb to pluck the bass notes on the lower three strings, and your index, middle, and ring fingers to pluck the 3rd, 2nd, and 1st strings, respectively.

- Fingernails, Flesh, and Fingerpicks: there are several ways you can pluck the strings with your fingers. Fingernails sound great and can provide a consistent, clean attack, but you'll need to keep them well-buffed and filed so they are smooth and curved naturally around the fingertips. Some players will use just the flesh of their fingertips to pluck; this has its advantages as well. The sound is less consistent, but warmer and more organic, plus you don't have the nail maintenance. Another alternative are a thumbpick and fingerpicks, similar to a banjo player. These create a consistent sound and don't require upkeep, but do take some time to get used to.

- Arpeggios: the chords in this song are all played as arpeggios. Keep your fret-hand fingers arched so they don't inadvertently bump or mute any other strings. It helps to keep your fret-hand thumb planted on the back of the neck, roughly in line with your middle finger. This classical position will help keep your fingers arched, while also facilitating the fretting of the dyads that occur throughout as well.

Time in a Bottle

Words and Music by Jim Croce

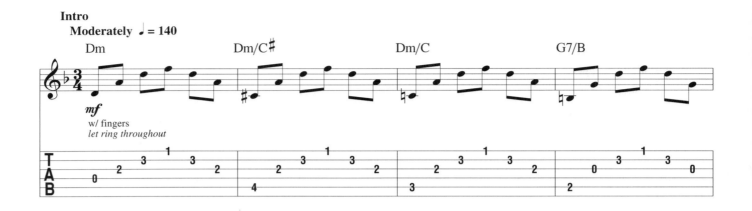

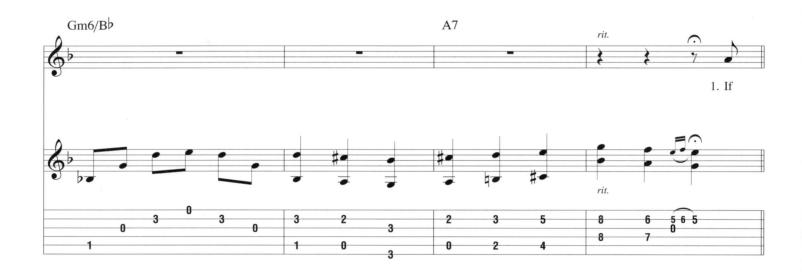

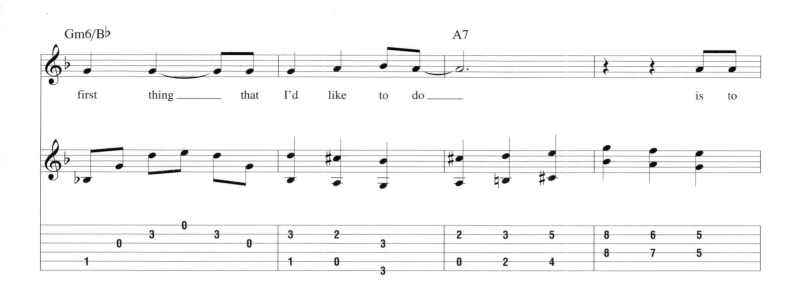

first thing_____ that I'd like to do_____ is to

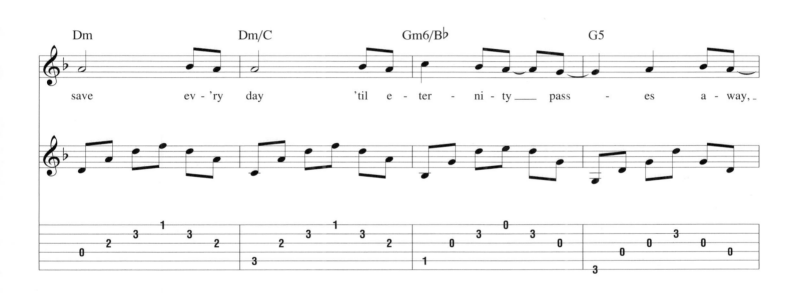

save ev - 'ry day 'til e - ter - ni - ty____ pass - es a - way,_

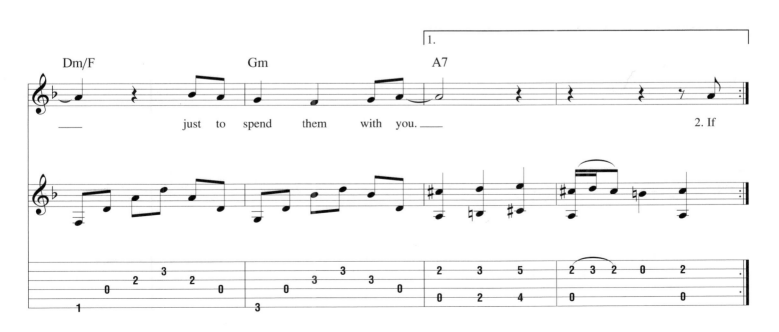

_____ just to spend them with you.____

2. If

Bridge

But there nev - er seems _____ to be e - nough time _____ to

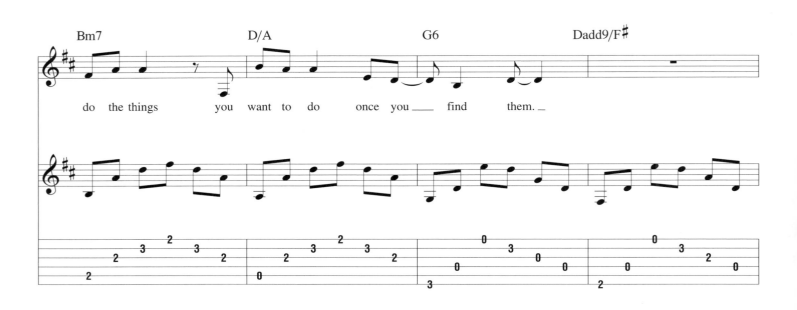

do the things you want to do once you ___ find them. _

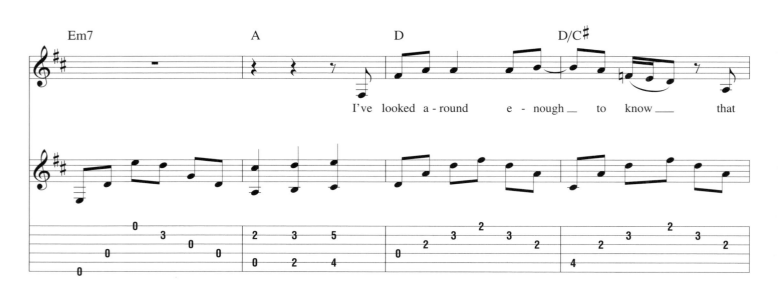

I've looked a - round e - nough ___ to know ___ that

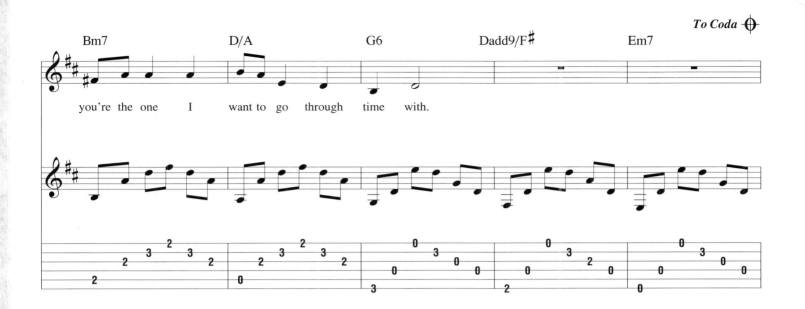

you're the one   I   want to go   through   time   with.

D.C. al Coda
(take 2nd ending)

⊕ **Coda**

Outro

Play 3 times

Harm. - - -|

Additional Lyrics

2. If I could make days last forever,
   If words could make wishes come true,
   I'd save ev'ry day like a treasure, and then
   Again I would spend them with you.

3. If I had a box just for wishes,
   And dreams that had never come true,
   The box would be empty except for the mem'ry
   Of how they were answered by you.

GUITAR NOTATION LEGEND

THE MUSICAL STAFF shows pitches and rhythms and is divided by bar lines into measures. Pitches are named after the first seven letters of the alphabet.

TABLATURE graphically represents the guitar fingerboard. Each horizontal line represents a string, and each number represents a fret.

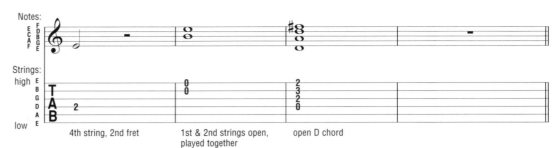

Notes:

Strings: high

low

4th string, 2nd fret

1st & 2nd strings open, played together

open D chord

HALF-STEP BEND: Strike the note and bend up 1/2 step.

WHOLE-STEP BEND: Strike the note and bend up one step.

GRACE NOTE BEND: Strike the note and immediately bend up as indicated.

SLIGHT (MICROTONE) BEND: Strike the note and bend up 1/4 step.

BEND AND RELEASE: Strike the note and bend up as indicated, then release back to the original note. Only the first note is struck.

PRE-BEND: Bend the note as indicated, then strike it.

VIBRATO: The string is vibrated by rapidly bending and releasing the note with the fretting hand.

PALM MUTING: The note is partially muted by the pick hand lightly touching the string(s) just before the bridge.

HAMMER-ON: Strike the first (lower) note with one finger, then sound the higher note (on the same string) with another finger by fretting it without picking.

PULL-OFF: Place both fingers on the notes to be sounded. Strike the first note and without picking, pull the finger off to sound the second (lower) note.

LEGATO SLIDE: Strike the first note and then slide the same fret-hand finger up or down to the second note. The second note is not struck.

SHIFT SLIDE: Same as legato slide, except the second note is struck.

TRILL: Very rapidly alternate between the notes indicated by continuously hammering on and pulling off.

TAPPING: Hammer ("tap") the fret indicated with the pick-hand index or middle finger and pull off to the note fretted by the fret hand.

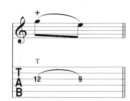

NATURAL HARMONIC: Strike the note while the fret-hand lightly touches the string directly over the fret indicated.

PINCH HARMONIC: The note is fretted normally and a harmonic is produced by adding the edge of the thumb or the tip of the index finger of the pick hand to the normal pick attack.

TREMOLO PICKING: The note is picked as rapidly and continuously as possible.

VIBRATO BAR DIVE AND RETURN: The pitch of the note or chord is dropped a specified number of steps (in rhythm), then returned to the original pitch.

VIBRATO BAR SCOOP: Depress the bar just before striking the note, then quickly release the bar.

VIBRATO BAR DIP: Strike the note and then immediately drop a specified number of steps, then release back to the original pitch.

Additional Musical Definitions

(accent) • Accentuate note (play it louder).

(staccato) • Play the note short.

D.S. al Coda • Go back to the sign (%), then play until the measure marked "***To Coda***," then skip to the section labelled "Coda."

D.C. al Fine • Go back to the beginning of the song and play until the measure marked "***Fine***" (end).

Fill

N.C.

• Label used to identify a brief melodic figure which is to be inserted into the arrangement.

• Harmony is implied.

• Repeat measures between signs.

• When a repeated section has different endings, play the first ending only the first time and the second ending only the second time.